the
POCKET
TEACHER

WIT AND WISDOM AT YOUR FINGERTIPS

BY TODD & JEDD HAFER

elevate

Some of the quotes and ideas in this book are inspired by teachings from the **Love and Logic**® Institute, Inc.

To learn more about **Love and Logic**® materials for parents, grandparents, and professionals, please visit:

www.loveandlogic.com or call: 1(800)338-4065.

A live person will answer Monday-Friday, 7am-5pm (MT).

Editorial Work: AnnaMarie McHargue

Cover Design: Aaron Snethen

Layout Design: Aaron Snethen

Published in Boise, Idaho by Elevate, an imprint of Elevate Publishing.

This book may be purchased in bulk for educational, business, organizational, or promotional use.

For information, please email info@elevatepub.com

Paperback ISBN-13: 9781943425228

eBook ISBN-13: 9781943425709

Library of Congress Control Number: 2015956301

Printed in the United States of America.

"Every child is one caring adult away
from being a success story."

Josh Shipp

INTRODUCTION:
TEACHERS TOUCH TOMORROW

Teachers. They are wise. They wear many hats. They can see behind their backs, around corners, and into the hearts and minds of the students they prepare for life.

A good teacher does not like to argue. He or she expects students to think, work, and learn. And knows kids shouldn't be spoiled or babied or bullied. Teachers prepare young minds for the world beyond the classroom. Teachers care unconditionally. And their words are pure gold.

Most of the time.

Yes, teachers are supposed to be reliable sources of life wisdom, often delivered with a wink and a clever turn of phrase. But let's face it—sometimes even the wisest educator can't bring the right words to mind, especially when the class is quarreling or begging to get out of an assignment or pop quiz.

Enter *The Pocket Teacher*, a handy source of inspiration, humor, and the right words—at just the right time. It's also a fun coffee table, break-room, or nightstand book that can be enjoyed for its simple entertainment value.

This book features classic quotes and come-backs from a variety of educators. These words reflect loving wisdom and rich life experiences, many of them inspired by the time-tested principles of the Love and Logic Institute, Inc., an invaluable resource for many, many teachers and parents (check out www.loveandlogic.com).

In the pages ahead, you'll encounter real-world scenarios and conundrums—each paired with an ideal teacher response—a response that is wise, effective, and loving. Because you cannot hear tone of voice in a book, it is important to remember that these phrases are meant to be said with sincere empathy and kindness, never sarcasm. The best teachers can communicate even difficult information with smiles and loving tones.

Additionally, blank pages allow any teacher to add his or her own signature phrases and classic words of wisdom, making this book a treasured, personalized keepsake as well as a handy reference.

We hope this book will be an engaging and enjoyable learning experience for you and those you love.

Jedd and Todd Hafer

Fix these words of mine in your hearts and minds. . .
Teach them to your children, talking about them when
you sit at home and when you walk along the road. . .
Write them on the doorframes of your houses and on
your gates. . .

Deuteronomy 11:18-20 NIV

THE SITUATION:

A student doesn't want to do an unpleasant task or assignment.

The teacher says...

"I know you don't like this, but thank you for doing it anyway. I really respect you for following through."

THE SITUATION:

Some students want to have pizza or some other treat, in class.

The teacher says...

"Great idea. Have you thought about how we can all earn it?"

THE SITUATION:
A student has used inappropriate language.

The teacher says...

"Can you think of a better way to say that?"

THE SITUATION:
A student is very upset and about to make a bad decision as a result.

The teacher says...

"I can tell you are mad. In the heat of emotion, we don't make the best decisions. Will you get back to me when you've had time to calm down and think things through?"

THE SITUATION:

A student is rebelling in the face of impending discipline (e.g., "I don't even care if you give me in-school suspension!")

The teacher says…

"Well, thank goodness. Now I won't have to feel so bad about it."

"A MAN FINDS JOY IN GIVING
AN APT REPLY—AND HOW GOOD
IS A TIMELY WORD!"

Proverbs 15:23 NIV

THE SITUATION:

A student says, "At my old school, we didn't have to do any homework!"

The teacher says…

"Well, I feel sad for the students at your former school. Aren't you glad that we expect more of you here?"

"WHEN TWO STUDENTS DISAGREE, FORCE THEM TO SHAKE HANDS AND SAY, 'I'M SORRY.' WHAT BETTER WAY TO GET TWO KIDS TO RESENT EACH OTHER?"

Tim Hanson

THE SITUATION:

A student complains, "I'm bored with your class."

The teacher says...

"Tolerating boredom is an essential life skill.
It's one I promise you will use."

THE SITUATION:

A student warns, "If you don't give me an A on this assignment, my parents are going to kill me!"

The teacher says…

"I like to travel, but I don't accept invitations for guilt trips."

THE SITUATION:

A student protests, "I don't want _____
as my lab partner. We don't get along."

The teacher says…

"You don't? That's good to know. What a great opportunity to
develop the skills of getting along with a challenging boss,
co-worker, or spouse!"

DID YOU KNOW?

According to the National Education Association, more than 7.2 million teachers (for grades K-12) are employed in U.S. public schools *alone*, and the need for new teachers continues to grow.

THE SITUATION:

A student is struggling to finish a difficult assignment.

The teacher says...

"Completing assignments is so important to lifelong success. So I can't let you off the hook. I need to stand firm this time, and YOU need me to stand firm."

"TEACHING IS THE ONLY JOB
WHERE YOU STEAL SUPPLIES
FROM HOME AND BRING THEM TO
WORK."

Marcia Edwards

THANK YOU FOR CALLING OUR SCHOOL...

To lie about why your child is absent today, press 1.

To offer an excuse for your child's late project
or low test score, press 2.

To leave an insult for the principal, press 3.

To swear at a teacher, press 4.

To ask why you didn't get the information that was emailed to you, snail-mailed to you . . . and that's available on the school's website and Facebook page, press 5.

To complain about the lack of parking spaces, press 6.

To ask when Christmas break begins, press 7
(or just check the calendar that's been posted on
our website since last summer).

To demand that your child gets a higher test grade, press 8.

To request a new teacher (for the third time this year),
press 9.

To demand that your child starts on the basketball team,
press 0.

If you would like to accept the reality that teachers and students and parents are imperfect people doing the best they can—and that, ultimately, students must be accountable for their behavior and importance, take a deep breath, hang up, and try to have a nice day!

THE FOLLOWING GRAPH
REPRESENTS THE CLASSROOM
EXPERIENCE FOR MANY OF THE
INDIVIDUALS DECIDING
CURRENT EDUCATION POLICY:

THE SITUATION:

A student won't take "No" (or "Yes") for an answer.

The teacher says…

"I care about you too much to argue. Please understand that my 'yes' means yes, and my 'no' means no."

"THE MORE A STUDENT'S
NASTY LOOKS OR MUMBLED
WORDS GET YOUR GOAT,
THE MORE YOUR GOAT
WILL BE GOT!"

H. J. Springston

"IF POLITICIANS HAD TO TAKE OR ADMINISTER STATE TESTS, THEY WOULD BE OUTLAWED IN FIVE MINUTES."

George House

THE SITUATION:

A student forgets to say please and/or thank you for a teacher's help or kindness.

The teacher says…

"I tend to do more things for people who say 'please' and 'thank you.'"

THE SITUATION:

A student protests, "You're not my parent; you're only my teacher!"

The teacher says...

"That's true. I am not your parent. But I am doing what I believe is right as your teacher, And I'll be happy to discuss that with all of us together."

10 COMMANDMENTS FOR TEACHERS:

1. It's good to make things fun, but don't get caught up in the belief that you must always entertain. The harder you work at entertaining your students, the more they will believe that they deserve to be entertained.

2. Always report your suspicions about students' disturbing behavior or threats. Always.

3. Always do the right thing, but know that it *won't always* be understood or appreciated.

4. Take care of yourself. That way, you will be better able to take care of your students.

5. Thou shalt never say, "I told you so!" Let the consequences speak for themselves.

6. Do not issue a reprimand until you are calm and have a solid plan in mind.

7. Teach in a way that creates the voice of wisdom in a student's head: "If I make a bad choice, I will suffer the consequences. And if I make a good choice…"

8. Realize that the best teaching tactics in the world won't work unless your students see that you practice what you preach.

9. Never let guilt guide your teaching.

10. Students will either live up to your highest expectations or down to your worst fears. So show them every day what you believe they will be.

THE SITUATION:

**A student is unhappy about a decision
(or school policy).**

The teacher says…

"I cannot convince you that my decision is fair. But I hope I
have convinced you that we both have to live with it."

THE SITUATION:
Every day, all the time.

The teacher says (with a philosophical air)…

"Life is precious, and the unexpected will happen.
Gives us reason to be as ready as we can be."

THE SITUATION:
A student needs advice.

The teacher says…

"I bet you can figure this out if you give yourself a chance. But let me know if you'd like some ideas."

THE SITUATION:

A student is complaining about "water under the bridge."

The teacher says...

"Complaining about yesterday will not make today one bit better. In fact, it might just make today worse."

"CONTROL IS A LOT LIKE LOVE;
THE MORE YOU GIVE AWAY, THE
MORE YOU RECEIVE."

Dr. Charles Fay

THE SITUATION:

A student is stirring up trouble for her- or himself.

The teacher says…

"If you're going to stir up a storm, please don't complain
when it starts to rain."

THE SITUATION:

A student is distraught over a poor report card.

The teacher says…

"I care about you, whatever grades you earn. But would you like some suggestions on how to make your next report card better?"

THE SITUATION:
A student is beaming over a great report card.

The teacher says...

"I care about you, whatever grades you earn. But I bet that feels great!"

"I ALWAYS PICTURE TEACHERS ON THEIR DEATHBEDS SAYING THINGS LIKE, 'JUST BRING ME MY STACKS OF MONEY AND EXPENSIVE JEWELS SO I CAN LOOK UPON THEM ONE LAST TIME!' OKAY, MAYBE NOT. BUT THEY HAVE INVESTED IN SOMETHING MUCH MORE VALUABLE—LIVES!"

Jedd Hafer

"JUST LIKE LOVE, SHARPIE MARKS ON THE CLASSROOM WALL ARE FOREVER."

George House

DID YOU KNOW?

When Betsy Alexander and Burnell Yow adopted Nora, a gray tabby, from a New Jersey animal shelter, they didn't know they were bringing home a musical prodigy. Alexander is a piano teacher, and Nora loved to sit near the piano when she gave lessons. One day, Nora decided to try her paws at the keyboard. She leaped onto the piano bench. The rest is Internet history. Her debut YouTube performance garnered more than 14 million views, and subsequent videos have been popular as well.

When she first discovered Nora's talent, Alexander sought answers from her local veterinary office. "I told them, 'She's playing the piano—what do you think?'" Alexander recalls. "They said, 'We don't know.'"

One animal behaviorist has theorized that Nora started playing the piano because she craved the attention Alexander was giving her students.

Incidentally, in 2009, Nora was named Cat of the Year by the ASPCA.

THE SITUATION:

A student is not paying attention to classroom instructions.

The teacher says…

"I can explain this to you, but I cannot understand it for you."

"I DON'T RECOMMEND DATING MATH TEACHERS...THEY HAVE TOO MANY PROBLEMS."

Todd Hafer

"YOU MUST BE A 90 DEGREE ANGLE, CUZ YOU ARE LOOKIN' RIGHT."

Geometry teacher pick-up line
(guaranteed not to work).

THE SITUATION:

A student is being mean to a classmate.

The teacher says…

[Scratching his/her head] "Do you remember when I asked you to be mean to your classmate? Neither do I."

THE SITUATION:
A student is complaining about lack of time for an assignment.

The teacher says...

"You get the same number of minutes in a day as world leaders, billionaire CEOs, and world-class athletes. It's all about using those minutes wisely."

THE SITUATION:
Some students are creating a problem for themselves.

The teacher says…

"As far as what you're doing? No problem—not for me, anyway. But what about for *you?*"

"THE PEOPLE WHO SAY
TEACHING IS AS EASY AS PIE
DON'T KNOW MUCH ABOUT
EDUCATION. OR PIE."

Todd Hafer

THE SITUATION:
**A teacher has (momentarily) forgotten
a student's name.**

The teacher says...

"I might have more students than I can name,
but not more than I can love!"

DID YOU KNOW?

Before becoming a world champion mixed martial arts fighter in the UFC, Rich Franklin was a high school math teacher in Cincinnati, Ohio. In fact, early in his career, Franklin held down both jobs, because teaching paid better than fighting.

THE SITUATION:

A student is worrying too much about something.

The teacher says…

"When we have a problem, we can either worry about it or do something about it. I cannot help you worry, but I *can* help you do something."

"NOT BY AGE BUT BY
CHARACTER IS WISDOM
ACQUIRED."

Titus Plautus

"CONSEQUENCES NEED TO BE MEANINGFUL AND SIGNIFICANT FROM THE GET-GO. YOU'LL HAVE FEWER PROBLEMS IN THE FUTURE."

Tim Hanson

THE SITUATION:

A student is justifying a feud with a classmate or teammate.

The teacher says...

"I have found that people in our school need consideration and kindness—especially when they don't deserve it!"

THE SITUATION:

A student is tempted to speak, act, or make a decision without thinking.

The teacher says…

"It's okay to take the time to think this over. Thinking is hard work, you know."

THE SITUATION:
A student is stuck in an emotional rut.

The teacher says…

"Sounds like you're not going to feel better until you decide to feel better."

DID YOU KNOW?

The U.S. Catholic parochial school system (8,500 strong) employs thousands of teachers, while thousands more instruct in various Protestant schools—totaling more than 7,000 in number. More than 2.7 million U.S. students attend a parochial school, and more than 4 million attend a Protestant religious school. All told, one U.S. student in 12 attends some type of religious school.

"THE VERY BEST WAY FOR STUDENTS TO SHOW THEY HAVE LEARNED ALL THE WONDERFUL THINGS I TEACH THEM? STANDARDIZED TESTS, OF COURSE."

No Teacher Ever

THE SITUATION:

The whole classroom seems to be stressed out.

The teacher says...

"Well, it seems that everyone is feeling miserable. But let's not make it into a competition."

"DOING THE RIGHT THING
FOR YOUR STUDENTS OFTEN
FEELS LOUSY AT THE TIME.
THE POSITIVE RESULTS AND THE
GOOD FEELINGS? THEY OFTEN
DON'T COME UNTIL LATER."

Abby Lopez

THE SITUATION:
Very rarely.

A wise teacher never says…

"Here's exactly what you need to do."
(A savvy teacher helps his or her students discover
solutions. He or she doesn't force-feed canned advice.)

THE SITUATION:

Everyday life.

The teacher says...

"I care about you very much! I am rooting for you!
I believe in you!"

(The above should be communicated
every day with words and actions.)

GOD SETS OUT THE ENTIRE
CREATION AS A SCIENCE CLASS-
ROOM, USING BIRDS AND BEASTS
TO TEACH WISDOM.

Proverbs 35:11 MSG

THE SITUATION:

A student does not get his or her way—
and protests mightily.

The teacher says...

"Not getting one's way is great practice for real life!"

DID YOU KNOW?

More than 1.5 million K-12 students are home-schooled, with a parent, friend, or relative serving in the teacher role. The number of home-schooled students has jumped 74 percent since 1999, and more and more local home-school associations are forming, with teams of specialized teachers sharing the duties of educating home-schooled kids in specific disciplines.

THE SITUATION:

A student is being loud and boisterous, across the classroom.

The teacher says, quietly, after approaching the student…

"Are you sure this is the right time and place for that kind of volume?" (A wise teacher realizes the inherent contradiction in shouting instructions to "Be quiet!" across the classroom.)

THE SITUATION:

**A student grumbles, "Why can't you give in—
just this once?"**

The teacher says...

"I don't give in. I don't make concessions. But I will allow you
to earn the right to do something different. Be respectful,
responsible, and creative with this matter, and let's see what
happens."

DID YOU KNOW?

Art Garfunkel (who came close to earning his Ph.D. in mathematics) was a prep-school math teacher. He maintained his teaching job (for a while) even after "Bridge Over Troubled Water" became a hit.

THE SITUATION:

A student protests, "Why do we have to do so much homework?"

The teacher says...

"The best person to answer that is you. Why do you think this much homework might be necessary?"

"I WOULD MUCH RATHER BE COLLECTING DATA THAN INTERACTING WITH MY STUDENTS."

No Teacher Ever

TO THE MOON, ALICE!

I took my rowdy third-grade class to a planetarium show ti-tled "A Trip to the Moon." We spent 27 minutes in the long, slow-moving line, as I tried to keep students from breaking ranks, removing their shoes for no apparent reason, and giving one another wedgies. My throat was raw from yelling things like, "Stevie, release that headlock right now!" At last, I made it to the box office window.

I smiled feebly at the cashier. "One adult ticket and 22 children for 'A Trip to the Moon,'" I rasped. "And, by the way, could you make those kids' tickets one way?"

Alice Randle
Grade school teacher, Denver, CO

THE SITUATION:

A student has responded to adversity by saying or doing something inappropriate (complaining, yelling, or throwing something).

The teacher says...

"I empathize with your feelings, but I cannot excuse your behavior."

"ONCE THEY WERE IN MY CLASS, I CALLED THEM 'MY KIDS' EVEN WHEN THEY WERE ALL GROWN UP."

Annie Burke

"IT'S EASY TO GET A STUDENT'S ATTENTION: JUST SIT DOWN AT YOUR DESK, AND TRY TO GET A LITTLE READING DONE."

Robin St. John

THE SITUATION:
**A student wants to open up about a problem,
but is struggling to do so.**

The teacher says…

"Hey, would you like to help me with a project?"
[or]
"I could use some exercise; want to take a
quick walk with me?"

(Students often talk about difficult issues when they are
interacting in some way with a caring teacher.)

THE SITUATION:

A student has priorities confused.

The teacher says...

"The main thing is to keep the main thing
the main thing!"

"BEING A TEACHER IS LIKE
BEING A GENERAL IN THE ARMY.
YOU HAVE TO PICK YOUR
BATTLES CAREFULLY."

Cherie Rayburn

"BEST ADVICE I EVER RECEIVED? 'BE CAREFUL ABOUT USING YOUR TEACHER VOICE OUTSIDE THE CLASSROOM.' OF COURSE, I DO IT ALL THE TIME ANYWAY."

Marcia Edwards

THE SITUATION:

A student is being ungrateful or careless about school equipment or supplies.

The teacher says…

"I think we should love the stuff God has given us. Never know when He might take it back."

"IT'S 3:30 P.M. I'LL JUST GO HOME AND RELAX."

No Teacher Ever

TEACHER DEFINITIONS:

- Kindergartener: A noise with dirt on it.

- Laminator: A blessed invention made necessary by kindergarteners.

- Unbreakable ruler: An instrument whose very name a fifth-grade boy will take as a personal challenge.

- Fable: A literary form mastered by students who are habitually late with their homework.

- School cafeteria: Large room where children share Twinkies, colds, and embarrassing family secrets.

- Teachers' Lounge: A place smelling of reheated lunches where war stories are exchanged and exactly ZERO lounging is done.

THE SITUATION:
Some students stall out during an assignment or special project.

The teacher says...

"I like you too much to fight with you about doing your work. Let's talk when you're done."

THE SITUATION:

Someone is jumping up and down on the teacher's last nerve. (A rare occurrence indeed.)

The teacher says…

"I think better when I'm calm. Let's talk about this later."

"YOUR STUDENT IS NOT ARGUING WITH YOU BECAUSE HE WANTS TO HEAR YOUR EDUCATIONAL WISDOM. HE IS ARGUING TO WEAKEN YOUR RESOLVE AND GET HIS OWN WAY. REMEMBER THIS, AND YOU'LL HAVE FEWER ARGUMENTS."

George House

THE SITUATION:

A student is creating lots of drama for her- or himself.

The teacher says...

[With a wink] "You know, when I get tired of all the drama, I tell myself to stop acting up."

"WHEN A STUDENT SAYS,
'I HATE YOU,' HE IS REALLY
SAYING, 'I AM TRYING TO
MANIPULATE YOU, AND I'M
ANGRY THAT IT'S NOT
WORKING!'"

Robert Lopez

THE SITUATION:

Multiple students are interrupting the teacher when he or she is trying to speak.

The teacher says…

"I can teach a whole class full of people, but I can converse with one person at a time, maximum."

THE SITUATION:
A student is feuding with a classmate, teammate, or someone else at school.

The teacher says…

"Have you tried treating that person the way you'd want them to treat you?"

"TEACHERS SHOULD MOONLIGHT AS COMPETITIVE EATERS. EVERY TEACHER I KNOW CAN FINISH A SANDWICH IN .3 SECONDS— WHILE SPRINTING TO THE COPIER."

Jedd Hafer

THE SITUATION:

A student expresses displeasure over detention, suspension, or some other form of discipline (e.g., "This stinks! I hate it!")

The teacher says…

"Okay. Well, I guess I know it's working. Trust me—in the long run, we'll both be glad this happened."

THE SITUATION:

A student is becoming argumentative while discussing an assignment or other matter.

The teacher says…

"I want to help you, but I cannot help you while you are arguing with me. And I will understand you better when your voice is calm like mine."

THE SITUATION:

A student is expressing angst over an upcoming test.

The teacher says…

"I can see you are stressed about this test. But study hard, do your best, and I'll grade fairly."

THE SITUATION:
A student misses an assignment deadline.

The teacher says…

"Would you like to come in after school today and finish this assignment, or do it at home tonight and bring it to me at the start of class tomorrow? I would hate to see you get zero credit."

THE SITUATION:

A student butts in with a question or comment during a lecture or conversation.

The teacher says…

"I answer questions when kids raise hands and wait their turn to speak."

"TELL ME AND I FORGET. TEACH ME AND I REMEMBER. INVOLVE ME AND I LEARN."

Benjamin Franklin

THE SITUATION:

A student reports another student is teasing him/her.

The teacher says. . .

"I bet that is tough. Would you like to hear how some other students have handled this problem?"

10 THINGS THEY MIGHT NOT HAVE TAUGHT YOU IN COLLEGE:

1. In teaching, more is not always better. Remember to pause and let things sink in. Allow students to think for themselves..

2. An emotionally charged student needs three things—empathy, space, and time to cool down.

3. The more students can control teachers and coaches through manipulation, the more out of control they will feel.

4. Minimum anger from the teacher yields the maximum opportunity for a student to think, empathize, and learn from a mistake.

5. Wise teachers show their students, every day, that good deeds bring you good results. And bad behavior brings nothing but trouble.

6. The way you handle student tantrums will shape how they deal with disappointment and anger for the rest of their lives—and how they will respond to authority figures.

7. There is nothing wrong with an agitated middle-schooler that reasoning won't aggravate!

8. A wise teacher asks for help with things like depression, substance abuse, and anger management.

9. Students who don't feel listened to or understood by their teachers will find alternatives, like the local drug dealer or some sketchy corner of the Internet.

10. You can't fix every student's problem, but you can listen and show empathy. Sometimes that's more important than the "fix."

"TEACHING IS NOT A LOST ART,
BUT THE REGARD FOR IT IS A
LOST TRADITION."

Jacques Barzun

THE SITUATION:

**A frustrated student complains,
"I just can't do it. I'm not smart enough!"**

The teacher says…

"Aren't you glad that I don't believe that?"

"THEY THAT GOVERN MOST MAKE
THE LEAST NOISE."

John Selden

"WISE TEACHERS PLUG ALL THE
HOLES BEFORE THEY LAUNCH
THE BOAT."

Jim Fay

"IF YOU ARE PLANNING FOR A YEAR, SOW RICE; IF YOU ARE PLANNING FOR A DECADE, PLANT TREES; IF YOU ARE PLANNING FOR A LIFETIME, EDUCATE PEOPLE."

Chinese Proverb

"KIDS MAY NOT REMEMBER
EVERYTHING YOU TAUGHT THEM,
BUT THEY WILL REMEMBER HOW
YOU MADE THEM FEEL LOVED."

Cherie Hafer

"I HAVE COME TO A FRIGHTENING CONCLUSION. I AM THE DECISIVE ELEMENT IN THE CLASSROOM. IT IS MY PERSONAL APPROACH THAT CREATES THE CLIMATE. IT IS MY DAILY MOOD THAT MAKES THE WEATHER."

Dr. Haim Ginott

"Walk with the wise and become wise."
Proverbs 13:20 NIV

ADD YOUR OWN WISDOM!

FOR MORE BOOKS
FROM THE HAFERS

VISIT WWW.ELEVATEPUB.COM

elevate
publishing

DELIVERING TRANSFORMATIVE MESSAGES
TO THE WORLD

Visit www.elevatepub.com for our latest offerings.

NO TREES WERE HARMED IN THE MAKING OF THIS BOOK.

OK, so a few did make the ultimate sacrifice.

In order to steward our environment, we are partnered with *Plant With Purpose*, to plant a tree for every tree that paid the price for the printing of this book.

To learn more, visit www.elevatepub.com/about

PLANT WITH PURPOSE | WWW.PLANTWITHPURPOSE.ORG